CIRCULAR WALKS
IN THE
PEAK PARK

by
William and Vera Parker
with maps by P. J. Williamson

5th Edition

Walks revised for this editon by Pat and Peter Tidsall,
with assistance from Marjorie Hodgkiss

FOLLOW THE COUNTRY CODE

Guard against all risk of fire
Fasten all gates
Keep dogs under proper control
Keep to paths across farm land
Avoid damaging fences, hedges and walls
Leave no litter
Safeguard water supplies
Protect wildlife, wild plants and trees
Go carefully on country roads
Respect the life of the countryside

The route maps are based upon the Ordnance Survey mapping with the permission of
The Controller of Her Majesty's Stationery Office. Crown Copyright 399531

ISBN 0 85100 0 92 4

© William and Vera Parker 2002

Printed in

DERBYSHIRE COU
Heritage House, Lod

INDEX OF WALKS

14	Calver	Haywood Car Park – Tumbling Hill – Upper Padley – Grindleford – Hay Wood	3	32
15	Castleton	Castleton – Hollowford Road – Hollins Cross – Losehill Hall	4	34
16	Eyam	Eyam – Sir William Hill Road – Eyam Moor – Jubilee Plantation – Highcliffe	$3^1/_2$	36
17	Eyam	Eyam – Riley Graves – Stoney Middleton	3	38
18	Grindleford	Sir William Hill – Bretton Clough – Nether Bretton	$3^1/_2$	40
19	Grindleford	Grindleford Station – Upper Padley – Hathersage Booths – Harper Lees	3	42
20	Hathersage	Surprise View Car Park – Millstone Edge – Hathersage – Derwent River – Padley Gorge	6	44
21	Hathersage	Hollin Bank Car Park – North Lees Estate – Dennis Knoll – Stanage Edge	3	46
22	Hathersage	Hathersage – Hazelford Hall – Eyam Moor – Stoke Ford – Highlow Wood	6	48
23	Hathersage	Hathersage – Offerton Hall – Callow Wood – Leadmill Bridge	$3^1/_2$	50
24	Hope	Hope – Oaker Farm – Fiddle Clough – Edale End – Guide Post – Fullwood Stile Farm	6	52
25	Hope	Hope – Brough – Farfield Farm – Killhill Bridge	3	54
26	Litton	Litton – Tansley Dale – Cressbrook Dale – Wardlow – Wardlow Mires	3	56
27	Pilsley	Pilsley – Hassop – Birchill Bank Wood	$3^1/_2$	58
28	Wormhill	Wormhill – Hargatewall – Peter Dale	4	60
29	Youlgreave	Moor Lane Car Park – Middleton – Bradford Dale – Youlgreave	3	62
30	Youlgreave	Moor Lane Car Park – Cales Dale – Lathkill Dale – Meadow Place Grange	5	64

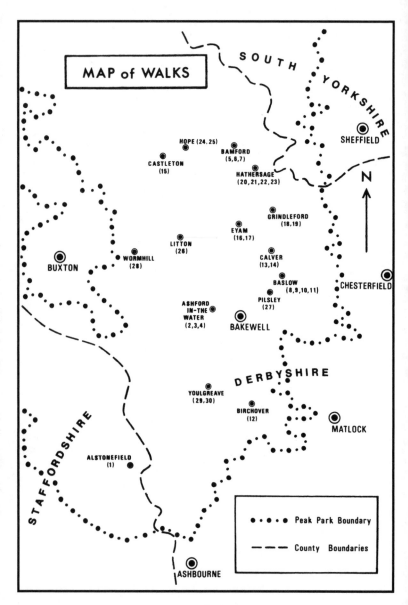

MAP of WALKS

SOUTH YORKSHIRE

SHEFFIELD

HOPE (24,25)

BAMFORD (5,6,7)

CASTLETON (15)

HATHERSAGE (20,21,22,23)

N

GRINDLEFORD (18,19)

EYAM (16,17)

LITTON (26)

WORMHILL (28)

BUXTON

CALVER (13,14)

BASLOW (8,9,10,11)

PILSLEY (27)

CHESTERFIELD

ASHFORD IN-THE WATER (2,3,4)

BAKEWELL

DERBYSHIRE

YOULGREAVE (29,30)

BIRCHOVER (12)

MATLOCK

STAFFORDSHIRE

ALSTONEFIELD (1)

•••• Peak Park Boundary

— — County Boundaries

ASHBOURNE

4

INTRODUCTION

The aim in writing this book is to put on record a collection of attractive short circular walks in the Peak Park in such a way that they may be easily followed. In this fifth edition all recent changes to the walks have been made and the instructions brought up to date.

A few of the walks are already popular, but this book includes many less well-known ones, which will lead you into parts of this lovely countryside which may be new to you.

Each walk is guided from the village named at the top of the page, and these villages are listed alphabetically. You are first given directions to the car park, and then led on the walk with clear instructions.

In the 'Walk Description' you will gain some idea of the nature of the walk, and what points of interest there are to be seen. Other useful information may be obtained from the Peak National Park Information Centres at The Old Market Hall, Bakewell; Fieldhead, Edale, and Castle Street, Castleton.

Although it is not necessary to use a map with this book, an Ordnance Survey Tourist Map 4 of the Peak District would add interest to your walks, and enable you to find easily the villages from which the walks commence.

In the Peak Park most of the footpaths and stiles are waymarked. A small yellow arrow sign indicates a footpath, and a blue arrow sign a bridleway, both of which may be used by walkers.

Although these walks are short, they often take you along rough stony footpaths and through muddy farms and fields. There are also some steep slopes. Stout footwear is essential, and ideally, boots and thick woollen socks should be worn. It should also be remembered that even on a short walk, cold and wet conditions can be experienced, and warm clothing and waterproofs should be part of your equipment.

All the walks in the book are along statutory footpaths and bridle-ways. As the years go by, landmarks, signposts and stiles may alter, and allowance for these changes should be made, as amendments can only be made in revised editions.

It is hoped that in following these walks, you will enjoy exploring, with ease and confidence, the beautiful countryside within the Peak Park.

ALSTONEFIELD – WALK 1   4½ MILES

Alstonefield – Coldeaton Bridge – Dovedale – Milldale – Hopedale – Alstonefield

STARTING POINT: Alstonefield Car Park.

PARKING: Alstonefield Car Park.
Directions from Buxton: Take the A515 Ashbourne road, and in 14 miles turn right at the signpost Alstonefield. In Alstonefield bear right on the Hulme End – Hartington road, signposted 'P Toilets' and the car park is immediately on your left. If this is full, turn round back up to the road junction and turn right to follow the new car park signs.
Directions from Ashbourne: Take the A515 Buxton road, and in 5 miles turn left at the signpost Alstonefield, then follow the directions above.

WALK DESCRIPTION: Dovedale is renowned for its beauty, and this walk takes you to the middle section between Wolfscote Dale and Milldale. Although you view the valley of the Dove at the beginning of the walk from the high viewpoint of the National Trust area 'Gipsy Bank', and descend very steeply to the Coldeaton Bridge, this is an easy walk, with only a very gradual ascent on the return journey. A one-mile walk along Dovedale leads you to the bridge at Lode Mill, and you then follow Mill Dale to the hamlet of Milldale. Here you can obtain refreshments at a country café beside the quaint Viator's Bridge, before continuing your walk. A one-mile road walk follows along a quiet valley, to the hamlet of Hope, where you follow lanes and fields back to Alstonefield.

ROUTE INSTRUCTIONS:

1. Turn right out of Alstonefield Car Park and bear left on the road to Lode Mill and Ashbourne.
2. Pass a 'Public Footpath' sign on the left and the decontrolled sign, then turn left at the signs for 'Youth Hostel' and 'Coldeaton Bridge via Gipsy Bank'.
3. Walk along a wide track passing the youth hostel. The track soon becomes much narrower. You will go round a right and then a left hand bend. At the end of the track (about ½ mile from the road) cross a stile into the National Trust area of Gipsy Bank.
4. Bear right, and descend the steep hill down a gully.
5. Cross the footbridge at the foot of the hill, and turn right along Dovedale.
6. Keep straight on beside the River Dove, and on reaching the road at Lode Mill, turn right over the bridge.

7. Take the first turn left signed 'Milldale ½', and at Milldale keep on the road, bearing right, signed 'P 300 yards'.

8. Follow this road for one mile to *The Watts Russell Arms*.

9. At the T-junction follow the road round the bend to the right and in 400 yards turn left on a walled lane. Pass Hope Green Farm on your right.

10. About 250 yards beyond Hope Green Farm and having passed two footpaths opposite each other, a footpath on the right, and gone down a small hill, turn right through a stile by a gate: this is opposite another stile on your left.

11. Cross three fields and two stiles. The first field has a wall on the left, then two fields with a wall on the right.

12. Cross a stile by a gate.

13. Follow a walled track, and on reaching a road, turn right to the car park.

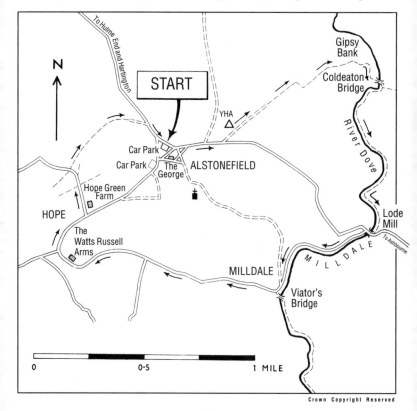

Crown Copyright Reserved

Monsal Head – Monsal Dale – Great Shacklow Wood – Ashford-in-the-Water – Monsal Head

STARTING POINT: Monsal Head Car Park.

PARKING: Monsal Head Main Car Park. Pay and Display.
Directions: From Ashford-in-the-Water take the B6465 Monsal Head - Wardlow road, and in 1½ miles turn left into the Car Park.

WALK DESCRIPTION: The starting point for this walk is at Monsal Head, the famous viewpoint overlooking Monsal Dale, where deep in the valley below, the River Wye curves from Upperdale to Monsal Dale, and passes under the viaduct which carried the now disused railway line from Bakewell to Buxton. The walk takes you into the valley and along a riverside path through Monsal Dale, to reach the road at Taddington Dale. An interesting undulating path through Great Shacklow Wood takes you to the A6 and into Ashford-in-the-Water, where you cross the ancient and picturesque Sheepwash Bridge, and return along walled tracks to see once more, from another angle, the superb view of Monsal Dale.

ROUTE INSTRUCTIONS:

1. From Monsal Head car park walk between the two parts of the Monsal Head Hotel. Turn left on the road, walk past the Monsal View Cafe and go through the top stile. Take the lower path downhill keeping a fence close on your right. Continue down the valley to the river.

2. Pass a weir, cross a footbridge, and bear left on the riverside path.

3. Near the end of the valley walk through the wood passing a FP post, cross two stiles and the main road to the White Lodge car park.

4. Follow the path up from the car park to cross a waymarked stile. In a few yards cross another stile and continue ahead passing a waymarked post on your right.

5. Follow a rocky path uphill to cross a stile. Pass the Bridleway sign to the A6 and White Lodge and the sign to Deep Dale. Continue on up the meandering shale path then stoney path towards the woods bearing left to cross a stile into the Great Shacklow Wood.

6. Follow the undulating woodland path for 1 mile ignoring all side paths.

7. Walk behind some old mill buildings down to the riverside path.

8. Follow the river on your left for about ½ mile crossing two stiles and ignoring all side paths.

9. Go through a small gate and along a short track to the minor road.

10. Keep straight on along the minor road to the A6

11. At the main road turn right, and in about 200 yards, turn left over the packhorse bridge into Ashford-in-the-Water.

12. Turn right along Main Street, passing the church and turn left at the signpost 'Monsal Dale B6465' on Greaves Lane.

13. In 100 yards turn left up Hill Cross, turn right at the T-junction, and in a few yards turn left into Highfields, enter a walled track signposted 'Footpath'.

14. Keep on the walled track. At the right bend follow the waymarked signpost 'Monsal Head'.

15. Near the end of the track pass an overgrown track on your right. Go over a stile. Walk up the field following the wall close on you left.

16. At the top of the field go through a gated stile and turn right. Walk past a dew pond and through another gated stile. Follow a walled path and through a stile. Keep straight on along the bottom of a field and go through another gated stile to enter the walled path again.

17. Go through a small gate to the viewing seat. Turn right to follow the wall on your right.

18. Continue along a well-used path towards Monsal Head. Go down steps and across a stile. As you near Monsal Head a path comes up from the left. Continue up to the road at Monsal Head.

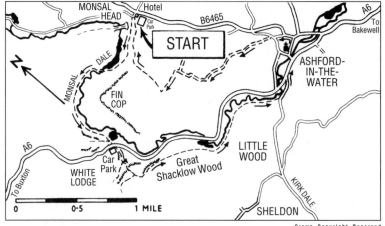

Crown Copyright Reserved

9

Monsal Head – Upperdale – Brushfield Hough – Monsal Dale – Monsal Head

STARTING POINT: Monsal Head Car Park. Pay and Display.

PARKING: Monsal Head Main Car Park.
Directions: From Ashford-in-the-Water take the B6465 Wardlow road, and in 1½ miles turn left into the car park.

WALK DESCRIPTION: The view of Monsal Dale from Monsal Head has been seen and admired by many visitors to the Peak Park, but the impressive view of the dale from the other side of the valley can be seen only on this walk. You first descend into Upperdale and cross the river and the railway track. On reaching the ridge, a slight diversion at Point 7 leads to an excellent viewpoint overlooking Monsal Dale. The walk continues through a farm at Brushfield Hough and down to Monsal Dale. A pleasant riverside walk leads you to the weir and up the hillside to Monsal Head

ROUTE INSTRUCTIONS:

1. From the Monsal Head car park, walk between the two parts of the hotel; *The Stables Pub* is on the left. Turn left on the road and opposite the *Monsal View Cafe* go through the largest of the three wall gaps. Turn right signed 'Access to Viaduct'.

2. Follow the steps downhill, ignoring steps off to the left, continue down to the cottage in the valley bottom.

3. Turn left by the cottage, cross the bridge and turn right to follow the sign 'Footpath to Brushfield and Taddington', keeping a fence close on your right.

4. At a stile (do not cross it) turn left crossing a railway bridge and a stile, and keep straight on with a fence on your right to another stile .

5. Keep straight on along the path, through scrubland. Turn left up the hill on a rough track.

6. Near the top of the hill go through a waymarked gate. Follow the track round a right hand bend and at a T-junction of tracks turn right up the hill.

7. At the top of the hill, pass through a waymarked gatepost and divert a few yards to the left for a magnificent view of Monsal Dale.

8. Return to the track and keep straight on for about ½ mile. Pass through a stile by a gate. Continue ahead keeping a wall on your left.

9. Cross another stile by a gate and in a few yards turn left over the wall stile by the footpath sign, 'Brushfield Hough'. Keep straight on across the field to go through a waymarked gate. Follow the track.

10. Pass through a gate and the farm. Just before the end of the buildings turn left through a waymarked gate to cross the yard. Turn right through another gate.

11. Go through a gateway onto the farm drive, and where the drive bends to the right, go over a stile on your left, by the 'Public Footpath' post.

12. Turn right, then bear left to follow a grass path through scrubland. Turn left on a more definite path down through scrub then woodland for about ¼ mile.

13. Near the bottom of the hill take the second left turn at a T-junction of paths. At the footpath post turn left signed 'Monsal Dale'.

14. Walk along Monsal Dale, and just before reaching the weir, bear right and cross the bridge; turn left to follow the river to the weir.

15. Follow the path up the hillside back to Monsal Head.

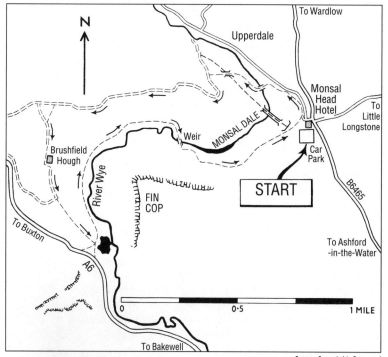

Crown Copyright Reserved

11

Monsal Head – Little Longstone – Wardlow – Cressbrook Dale – Ravensdale – Upperdale – Monsal Head

STARTING POINT: Monsal Head Car Park.

PARKING: Monsal Head Main Car Park. Pay and Display.
Directions: From Ashford-in-the-Water take the B6465 Wardlow road, and in 1½ miles turn left into the car park.

WALK DESCRIPTION: If you take this walk in late October, the wide bank of trees on the steep-sided slopes of Cressbrook Dale makes a lovely picture, with the trees in their glorious autumn colours. But this walk is rewarding at any time of the year, with its superb views over Monsal Dale, Upperdale and Cressbrook Dale. On the first part of the walk you slowly ascend the hillside from Monsal Head, where, on looking back, you have a good view of Great Longstone, Monsal Dale, Upperdale, and the spire of Bakewell church. After leaving Wardlow you soon reach a magnificent viewpoint over Cressbrook Dale, with Tansley Dale leading off to the village of Litton. At Ravensdale Cottages climbers can often be seen on the sheer cliffs of the impressive Bull Tor crags. An easy walk follows, on a quiet road through Upperdale, but there is a very steep climb at the end of the walk back to the elevated viewpoint at Monsal Head.

ROUTE INSTRUCTIONS:

1. Leave the Monsal Head car park by the main entrance, cross the road, and follow the road signposted 'Great Longstone'.

2. In ¼ mile, at Little Longstone, turn left on the footpath beside *The Pack Horse Inn,* signed 'Public footpath to Chertpit Lane'.

3. Pass on the right of a breeze-block building and keep straight on for 50 yards. Go over a stile to the left of a field gate and bear right.

4. In 100 yards turn right over a stile, and immediately turn left, keeping by the wall on your left.

5. Cross a stile, bear right across the centre of a field, cross a stile at a wall corner signposted 'Footpath'.

6. Walk diagonally up the field passing a stone barn over on your left and aiming for a wall corner. Cross the wall stile

7. Keep straight on following a broken wall on your left and gradually veering right to follow a 'good' wall on your right. Continue in a northerly direction keeping close to the wall on your right and crossing two stiles.

8. Bear left across the field to a stile, and turn right on a track.

9. In a third of a mile turn left over a stile by a gate signed 'Picnic Area' and cross another stile immediately on the left and follow the track uphill.

10. At the top of the hill bear right between a wall and old fence posts, and cross a stile on your left.

11. Keep straight on down the field heading for the road. Notice a conical hill half left in the middle distance. Cross a stile by a gate, a farm track and a Footpath sign.

12. Turn right along the road keeping straight on at a crossroads.

13. After about ¾ mile on the road, before reaching *The Bull's Head*, after a 40mph sign and opposite 'The Barn', turn left signed 'Public Footpath to Ravensdale'.

14. Follow a walled path and at the second righthand bend go through a squeeze stile.

15. Walk up a very narrow field to cross a stile onto the English Nature area in Cressbrook Dale.

16. Bear left to follow the path to a wall corner. Continue along the path as it winds its way along the valley side, then gradually descends through the woods. Ignore a path coming in on the right.

17. Cross a plank bridge, continue along the dale with a wall on your left. Eventually pass Ravensdale Cottages and continue up the lane.

18. On reaching the road, turn left, and keep straight on into Upperdale (nearly 1 mile).

19. Keep straight on at the crossroads at the signpost 'Monsal Head'.

20. At the 'Steep hill' sign bear right on a track, to the waymarked sign 'Bridleway Monsal Head'. Climb up the valley back to the car park.

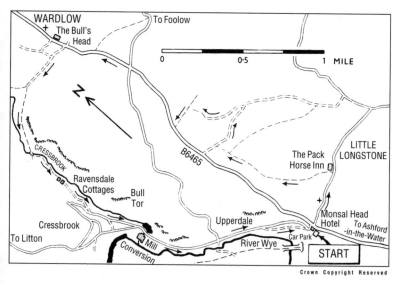

Crown Copyright Reserved

Cutthroat Bridge – Derwent Moor – Whinstone Lee Tor – Ladybower Tor – Cutthroat Bridge

STARTING POINT: Lay-by on the A57, near Cutthroat Bridge 1¼ miles north-east of the Ladybower reservoir viaduct.

PARKING: As above.
Directions from Bamford: With Bamford Church on your right, follow the A6013 for 2 miles, and turn right at the T-junction, signpost Sheffield A57. In one mile turn right into a large lay-by.

WALK DESCRIPTION: As you walk across the quiet moor leading to Derwent Edge, ignore the call of the grouse 'Go back – go back' and continue along the path, with its wide view of the Bamford valley and Win Hill. At Derwent Edge a magnificent view suddenly appears – the lakeland of the Peak Park – where the Ladybower reservoir, which flooded the village of Ashopton, has merged into the countryside, and enhanced, rather than detracted from the natural beauty of this lovely area. Over to the right, beyond the Ladybower reservoir, but not in view at this point, lie the Derwent and Howden reservoirs. From your viewpoint you see in the distance Lose Hill and Mam Tor. The humped Crook Hill is in the middle distance, with the elongated plateau of Kinder Scout beyond. At Whinstone Lee Tor the walk continues down a steep path before it returns over the moors. You may reflect that on this walk you have been rewarded with superb views in return for very little effort.

ROUTE INSTRUCTIONS:

1. Turn left out of the lay-by, walk down the road for 200 yards, cross Cutthroat Bridge, and immediately turn right.

2. Follow the main moorland path, which soon bears left in a steady easy ascent for just over 1 mile.

3. At a crossing of six paths near Whinstone Lee Tor, keep straight on for 50 yards to a viewpoint.

4. Return to the crossing of paths and turn very sharp left down a steep grass and stone path with the National Trust sign on your right.

5. Continue to follow the path downhill first with a wall, and then a wall and plantation, on your right. Keep straight on through the woodland.

6. At the end of the wood go through a small gate on your right. Turn left and pass through another gate.

7. Walk along a narrow undulating bracken-edged path with the reservoir on your right.

8. Eventually pass through a gate and walk behind the Ladybower Inn.

9. On reaching a wide track, bear left uphill. Go through a gate and continue uphill.

10. At a Y-junction of paths, keep straight on on the lower path.

11. Cross a stream, go through a gate, and keep straight on by the power lines.

12. At another Y-junction of paths by the powerline pole, take the left fork which is nearly straight on. In a few yards you join a wider path. Turn sharp right to retrace your route back to the car.

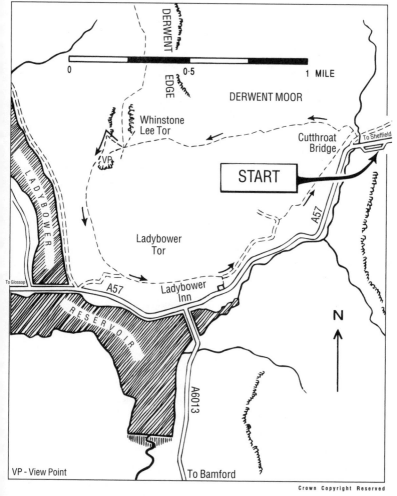

Crown Copyright Reserved

Ladybower Reservoir – Grindle Barn –
Whinstone Lee Tor – Ladybower Reservoir

STARTING POINT: Ladybower reservoir viaduct.

PARKING: Pull-in near a telephone box on the eastern side of the Ladybower
viaduct.
Directions from Bamford: With Bamford church on your right,
follow the A6013 for 2 miles, and turn left at the T-junction traffic
lights (signpost A57 Glossop). In ¼ mile bear left into pull-in near
a telephone box before the viaduct.

WALK DESCRIPTION: Beneath the viaduct at the start of this walk lies the
village of Ashopton, which was flooded in the 1930s by the newly constructed
Ladybower reservoir. It was feared at the time that the intrusion of this artificial
reservoir would destroy the natural beauty of Derwent Dale, but as you walk
along the shore-path, you will realise that these fears were unfounded. Leaving
the reservoir, you climb to the 300-year-old Grindle Barn, and walk across
moorland to a path on the slopes of Derwent Edge. Passing by a rocky ridge,
Whinstone Lee Tor, you descend a path from Whinstone Lee Gap to your
starting point.

ROUTE INSTRUCTIONS:

1. At the western end of the lay-by cross the road and follow a private drive
signed 'Footpath'.
2. In 100 yards pass through a swing gate at signpost 'Public bridleway
Derwent'.
3. In 1 mile, at a hairpin bend, keep straight on through a swing gate.
4. In ¼ mile, go through another gate and immediately turn right through a
small gate signed 'Bridleway'.
5. Follow a stone slabbed path up to Grindle Barn. Go through a gate and
walk round the barns to go through another gate.
6. Follow a path which turns right to cross a stream.
7. Follow the rocky footpath signposted 'Moscar', keeping a wall on your right.
8. Go through a gate and follow the path uphill with a wall still on your right.
9. Go through a gate and continue uphill to walk between a wall and a fir
wood.
10. Pass through a gate and bear right up the moorland bridleway, heading for
a wall and gate.

11. Go through the gate and turn right. In a few yards pass the Moscar sign to continue along the Bridleway with the wall on your right heading for Whinstone Lee Tor.

12. Keep the wall on your right all the way until you pass beneath the rocks of Whinstone Lee Tor. At a meeting of six tracks at Whinstone Lee Tor, turn very sharply right down a steep grass and rock track.

13. Follow the path, first with a wall, and then a plantation, on your right.

14. Continue through the woodland. You will see part of a broken wall on your left then further on a fence and wall on your right.

15. Go through a small gate on your right and turn right onto a wide track.

16. Go through a gate. Shortly you will reach a metalled road near houses.

17. Follow the hairpin bend round to your starting point.

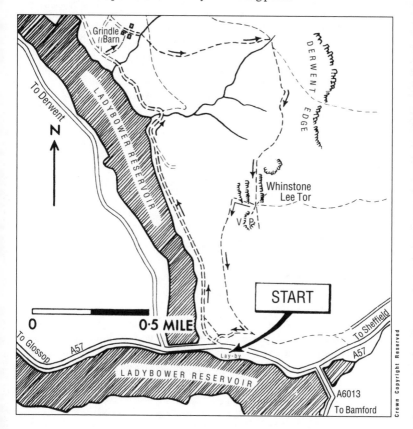

Snake Road – Crookhill Farm – Crook Hill – Grimbocar Wood – Snake Road

STARTING POINT: Snake road lay-by parking.

PARKING: Snake road lay-by parking.
Directions from Bamford: With Bamford church on your right, continue along the A6013 over the viaduct, and at the T-junction traffic lights turn left onto the A57 and go over the Ladybower viaduct. The car park is on the right in ½ mile.

WALK DESCRIPTION: This is a walk around Crook Hill, which rises in the angle between the road to Derwent and the Snake Pass road. As you ascend the hillside to Crookhill Farm, you have a superb view of Derwent Edge and Stanage Edge. After passing by the farm you soon see Crook Hill on your left, and experience the quietness of these remote hills, where you may have only the sheep for company. Fine views of Kinder Scout and Lose Hill open up as you ascend the hillside. You descend through woodland to the Snake road where, in order to make this a circular walk, some road walking is necessary but you will no doubt enjoy the one-mile walk alongside the Ladybower reservoir in its picturesque setting of fir plantations which rise on all sides.

ROUTE INSTRUCTIONS:

1. Turn left out of the car park in the direction of Sheffield and in nearly ½ mile turn left at the signpost 'Derwent Valley'.

2. In 100 yards turn left through a gate, signposted 'Footpath to Crookhill Farm'.

3. Keep straight on up with the National Trust fence on your right. At the fence corner keep straight on up the bank.

4. Walk diagonally right up the field and go over a stile by a gate in the top right-hand corner.

5. Continue uphill with the wall on your right and then cross a ladder stile.

6. Turn right to go through a gate as indicated by the National Trust signs. Turn left to walk up the field to the right-hand end of a barn, then behind the barn to go through two small gates, across the drive and through a larger gate.

7. Walk diagonally up the field to go through a farm gate in the top right corner.

8. Turn right onto the farm track signed 'Bridleway to Rowlee' and gradually climb keeping the wall on your right. Pass through another gate and continue ahead still with the wall on your right.

9. Shortly bear left away from the wall by a blue waymarked post.

10. Continue uphill following the line of these waymarked posts until you reach a gate (do not go through it).

11. Turn back on yourself to follow the 'Snake Road' sign. Keep the wall on your right to pass through a small gate in the field corner. Continue ahead keeping the wall on your right and Crook Hill on your left.

12. Before you reach the bottom corner of the field and at a gate and waymarked post on your right bear off left across the field corner to the Bridleway sign. Turn right to go through a gate.

13. Descend the track down through Grimbocar Wood to the Snake road, where you turn left and walk along the roadside footpath for one mile to the car park.

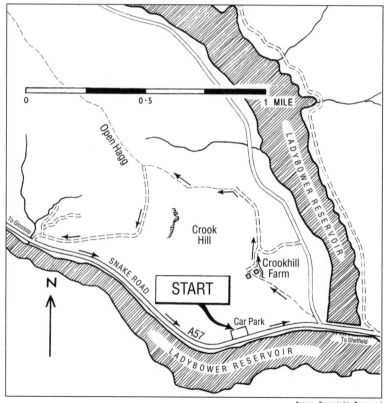

Crown Copyright Reserved

Birchen Edge Car Park – Birchen Edge – Wellington's Monument – Gardom's Edge – Birchen Edge Car Park

STARTING POINT: Birchen Edge Car Park, near Baslow.

PARKING: Birchen Edge Car Park, near Baslow.
Directions from Baslow: Leave Baslow on the Sheffield road A621, and at the first junction turn right onto the A619 Chesterfield road. In one mile turn left onto the B6050 Cutthorpe road, and immediately left into Birchen Edge Car Park.

WALK DESCRIPTION: Birchen Edge is a rather sombre gritstone ridge, on moorland lying adjacent to the Chatsworth Estates. On the top of the Edge is Nelson's Monument, and you may wish to climb from the path you take along the foot of the rocks to see the monument and the striking view from there of Baslow and Chatsworth Park. Continuing along the rocky lower path, you cross moorland, which in wet weather can be boggy in parts, to the Sheffield to Baslow road. From here you walk through lightly wooded countryside, on a track which was the old road to Chesterfield, and there is a stone on the track carved with the words 'Chesterfeild Roade'. From the high viewpoint at Wellington's Monument there is a fine view of Baslow and Chatsworth Park from another angle. You descend from the monument to the Baslow road again, and climb moorland paths beneath Gardom's Edge to yet another magnificent viewpoint. On your final descent you have a view of Birchen Edge, Nelson's Monument, and the three rocks known as 'The Three Ships'.

ROUTE INSTRUCTIONS:

1. Leave the car park, turn left along the B6050 and in 100 yards turn left up a bank and through a gate to follow wide steps uphill. Turn left along the hillside with a golf course on your left.

2. At the second junction of paths bear right, keeping to the main path, up the hillside, and bear left at the foot of Birchen Edge. Follow the Edge, passing below Nelson's monument.

3. At the northern end of Birchen Edge follow the main path which bears slightly left down the hill away from the Edge. Cross the marshy moorland to a road seen in the distance (path not on O.S. 2½" map).

4. Cross a stile by the crossroads, cross the A621 and follow the minor road. Turn left in 150 yards through a small gate onto a wide track.

5. After about ¾ mile, at Wellington's Monument, continue along the track to a T-junction of paths. Turn left down a wide stony track. Before reaching a gate across the track turn sharp left along a narrow path with a wall and fence on your right.

6. Follow the boulder strewn path through a wood, as it descends steeply downhill, with a wall on your right. As you near the bottom of the hill the path curves left round a marshy area.

7. Go over a stile along a narrow walled and fenced path. Cross a footbridge. To the left is a most interesting garden.

8. Turn right through a wall gap to follow the 'garden' path and through another wall gap. Walk up to a stile and the main road.

9. Cross the road and go over the stile opposite. Follow a path which goes diagonally right over another stile to follow a fence on your right, then bear left uphill towards Gardom's Edge.

10. Go through a gap in a wall ahead and continue to follow the path uphill through a wood.

11. At the top of the hill, cross a wall and follow the path, with a wood on your right.

12. Follow this path keeping the wood on your right until it veers left on a grass track above the road.

13. Follow a grass track down the hillside in the direction of a road to be seen in the distance.

14. At the bottom left-hand corner of the pasture-land, cross a stile onto the main road, turn left for 200 yards, and turn left to the car park.

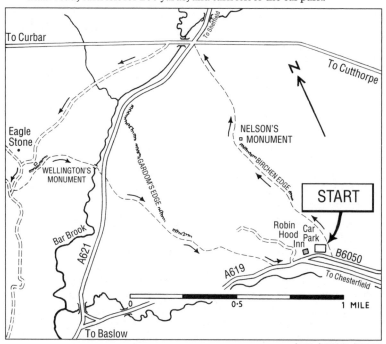

Crown Copyright Reserved

BASLOW – WALK 9   5 MILES

Chatsworth Park – Beeley – Burnt Wood –
Beeley Moor – Beeley Hilltop – Chatsworth Park

STARTING POINT: Calton Lees Car Park, Chatsworth Park, near the southern entrance.

PARKING: Calton Lees Car Park, Chatsworth Park.
Directions: To reach the car park from Baslow, take the A619 Bakewell road, and in $^1/_2$ mile keep straight on the B6012 Matlock road to Chatsworth Park. Drive through the park to the far end, keeping on the main road. The car park is on your right, just after crossing a cattle grid.

WALK DESCRIPTION: You will find this walk interesting, scenic and perhaps a little different from the valley and hill walks in the more popular areas of the Peak Park. From the Calton Lees Car Park in Chatsworth Park, you cross the fields to Beeley, a pretty village with attractive cottages. A short walk through fields and past farms brings you to Burnt Wood, where there is a large disused quarry. Passing by a small waterfall you reach a quiet meadow by a stream. A level walk through fields, with Fallinge Edge and Raven Tor on your right, leads to a minor road and a stony track, which takes you through the hamlet of Beeley Hilltop back to your base.

ROUTE INSTRUCTIONS:

1. From the car park walk to the driveway down to the Garden Centre. A few yards down the driveway turn left onto a path then almost immediately right. Walk down through the woods to the Park road.

2. Turn right, cross a bridge, and at the end of the bridge turn right through a kissing gate.

3. Cross a large field to a kissing gate near Beeley church, cross the road, and proceed along the minor road opposite, passing the church on your left.

4. At the T-junction turn right, and bear left at the fork of roads.

5. Just before the 'No-through Road' sign take the first turn right, and then straight on, on a footpath across a stream and a gated stile.

6. Follow the meandering path uphill (do not enter the wood). Go through a gap by the stile.

7. Keep straight on across the field, pass through a kissing gate, cross the road and through a gated stile. Follow the path, with a fence on your right.

8. Go through a gate ahead of you. Continue straight on following the waymarked arrow. At the end of the next field turn right over a stile by a gate and turn left to go through two more stiles, with a wall on your left.

9. Keep straight on through a small copse then through a gate. Continue in the same direction crossing two fields and two stiles.

10. Two-thirds of the way across the next field, cross a stile on your left, and turn right to another wall stile.

11. Walk beside the hedge on your right to a stile in the field corner (waymarked). Turn left up a walled path, ignoring a gate on the right.

12. At the top of the path bear left up through Burnt Wood.

13. In 100 yards, at a T-junction with another path, turn right, continuing up through the wood. In 200 yards pass between high stone built buttresses.

14. Near a small waterfall and a bridge down on your right bear left on the main path passing a quarry on your left. Leave the wood via a gate to follow the stream on your right. Ignore a wall stile on your left.

15. At a T-junction with a farm track turn left up the bridleway past a barn and through a squeeze stile by a gate.

16. Follow the track for nearly 1 mile to the road.

17. On reaching the road, turn right.

18. In just over ½ mile, where the road bends right, turn left. Follow the track for just over 1½ miles ignoring all other side paths and tracks. You will pass through the hamlet of Beeley Hilltop after which the track becomes a surfaced road.

19. On reaching the road, turn right.

20. Cross the bridge, and bear left on a footpath up the bank back to the car park.

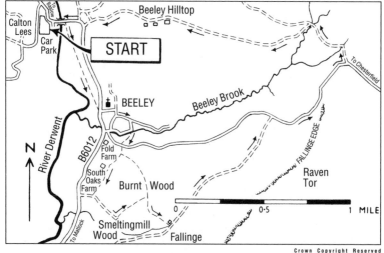

Crown Copyright Reserved

23

Baslow – Bank Wood Ridge – Bramley Farm – Bubnell – Baslow

STARTING POINT: Baslow Car Park. Pay and Display

PARKING: Baslow Car Park, adjacent to *The Cavendish Hotel*, on the Nether End (east) side of Baslow.

WALK DESCRIPTION: Bank Wood Ridge overlooks the Calver to Hassop road, and the walk along this high ridge gives views in the Longstone Edge direction. You leave Baslow on the old packhorse bridge over the River Derwent, and follow footpaths up the hillside, where, on looking back you see the rocky escarpment of Froggatt, Curbar and Baslow Edges. In the distance lies Chatsworth House, and on a clear day you may be able to see the Hunting Tower, which lies just below the skyline. A three-quarter-mile walk along a minor road brings you to Bank Wood Ridge, where you have a view on your right of Bramley Dale and Baslow. A quiet farm lane leads you through the hamlet of Bubnell, with its seventeenth century Bubnell Hall, and along the riverside, past an attractive weir, to the bridge leading back to Baslow.

ROUTE INSTRUCTIONS:

1. Turn left out of Baslow car park, and with *The Cavendish Hotel* on your left, walk along the main road and bear right at the junction.

2. Just past Baslow church turn left over the bridge, signed 'Bubnell'.

3. At the end of the bridge cross the road, and go through a stile between cottages.

4. Cross a stile, and pass through three fields, with a wall on your right.

5. Cross a stile, and where the wall bends to the right, turn left across the field.

6. Cross a stile by a gate.

7. Turn right along the road for nearly 1 mile, and 100 yards beyond the point where the road descends, turn right over a stile by a gate, a fence and a footpath sign.

8. Turn left to walk up the field following a wall on the left. Cross a stile into the wood. (From here to the lane it is about ¾ mile).

9. Follow the undulating woodland path with the wall on your right. Pass through a gate into an open area of bracken.

10. Continue along the ridge going through two small gates and keeping the wall on your right.

11. Continue to follow the path through the wood.

12. Go through the third gate on your right and turn left down a wider path for about 90 yards. Cross the stile by a gate.

13. Turn right down a lane, bearing right at Bramley Farm.

14. Follow the lane through Bubnell for ¾ mile and turn left over the bridge.

15. Turn right at the main road, and bear left onto the Sheffield road back to the car park.

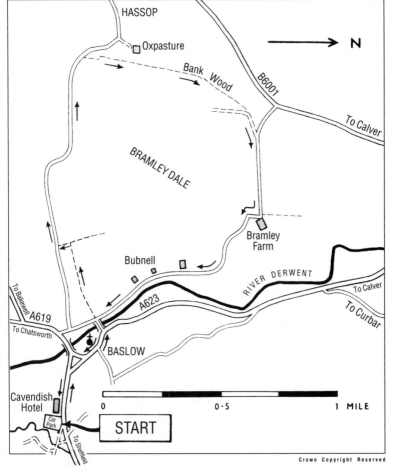

Crown Copyright Reserved

BASLOW – WALK 11   5½ MILES

Baslow – Pilsley – Edensor – Chatsworth Park – Baslow

STARTING POINT: Baslow Car Park. Pay and Display

PARKING: Baslow Car Park, adjacent to *The Cavendish Hotel*, on the Nether End (east) side of Baslow.

WALK DESCRIPTION: This walk enables you to visit the attractive Chatsworth Estate villages of Pilsley and Edensor (pronounced Ensor). From Baslow you cross the packhorse bridge near the church, and follow field paths to Pilsley. After climbing a country road, you descend a sunken lane to Edensor, the model village of the Chatsworth Estates. The original village could be seen from Chatsworth House, and in the opinion of the fourth Duke of Devonshire, this spoiled the view. It was therefore demolished in the eighteenth century, and the new village, with its elegant dwellings, was built in its place. You continue the walk past Queen Mary's Bower, where the Queen of Scots, who was kept a prisoner at Chatsworth House, spent some of her time in the open air. You complete your walk along the riverside path back to Baslow.

ROUTE INSTRUCTIONS:

1. Turn left out of Baslow car park, and with *The Cavendish Hotel* on your left, walk along the main road and bear right at the junction.

2. Just past Baslow church turn left over the bridge, cross the road, and go through a stile between cottages.

3. Walk up a narrow stone path to cross a stile. Keep straight on crossing three fields and three stiles and keeping a wall close on your right.

4. In the fourth field, where the wall turns right, turn left across the field to cross a stile by a gate.

5. Turn right on the lane for 70 yards, and turn left through a stile by a gate.

6. Follow the wall on your left, which turns first right and then left. 100 yards after the left turn in the path, cross a stile by a gate in a field corner.

7. Walk diagonally right down the field passing under power lines. Cross a stile and a footbridge.

8. Cross the main Baslow to Bakewell road through two stiles, and climb the steep hillside diagonally right towards the right hand side of a walled copse.

9. Cross a wooden stile, and immediately turn left, to follow a wall on your left.

10. Go over a stile onto a minor road, and turn right.

11. On entering Pilsley turn right past *The Devonshire Arms*, and go up the 'No Through Road'.

12. At the end of the houses, keep straight on along a track, and turn left at the Y-junction.

13. At the end of the walled lane turn left over a stile and cross a field to another stile.

14. Cross a road and keep straight on along a narrow road.

15. In ¾ mile, near the top of the hill, where the lane levels out and before it starts climbing again, turn sharp left at a red waymarked sign, on an unsurfaced track.

16. At the bottom of the ¾ mile track enter Edensor village and keep straight on through the main gates.

17. Cross the road, and follow a path which bears right along the hillside opposite, going over the hill, and descending to the bridge near Chatsworth House.

18. Cross the bridge, immediately turn left on the riverside path, with Queen Mary's Bower on your right and keep straight on the main track for one mile, the last part of which is unsurfaced.

19. Go through the tall black kissing gate.

20. Follow the track past houses and cottages and through a gate. Turn left over the bridge and left to the car park.

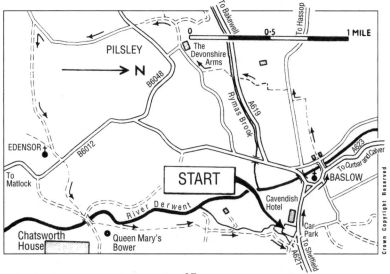

Crown Copyright Reserved

Birchover – Stanton Moor –
Nine Ladies Stone Circle – Birchover

STARTING POINT: Birchover.

PARKING: In Birchover. No official car park.
Directions from Bakewell: Take the A6 Matlock road for 2 miles,
turn right on the B5056 Ashbourne road, and in 1 mile turn left –
still on the B5056. In 1¼ miles turn left, to reach Birchover in ½
mile.

WALK DESCRIPTION: Birchover, from where this walk commences, lies high
on a hill near Stanton Moor. Behind *The Druid Inn* it is possible to clamber around
the Rowtor Rocks, where a local parson, long since deceased, hewed armchairs
and seats in the curiously-shaped rocks, from which to admire a view now
obscured by trees. You ascend from the village to Stanton Moor, a bronze-age
burial ground, where numerous barrows, or burial mounds, were discovered,
containing bronze-age vessels and implements. From the edge of the moor you
have a superb view in the Chatsworth direction, and you pass a tower which
commemorates the passing of the Reform Bill. At the northern end of the moor lies
the Nine Ladies Stone Circle – a circle of nine upright stones, believed to have been
constructed about 1500 B.C., and to have been used for religious festivals. The
King's Stone lies a short distance away. A level moorland walk, passing a curiously-
shaped rock, with metal rungs for climbing, brings you back to Birchover.

ROUTE INSTRUCTIONS:

1. With the *Red Lion* on your left, walk up the main street. Keep straight on up
   the hill out of the village, passing Barn Farm on your right.

2. Where the main road bends left bear right along the minor road with the
   quarry on your left.

3. Follow this minor road for just under ¼ mile and shortly after passing a
   footpath sign on your right turn left over a stile onto the moorland.

4. In 150 yards, at a junction of tracks, bear right.

5. On reaching a stile on your right below a rock mound, cross the stile onto the
   National Trust land and turn left to follow a path for about ½ mile, keeping
   the fence on your left.

6. At a T-junction turn left still with a fence on your left. Walk through the trees.
   At a fork of paths take the lower right fork to walk below a stone tower.

7. Keep to the main track, which eventually bears left over a stile, and in 80 yards
   turn left at a T-junction of paths.

8. 'The Nine Ladies Stone Circle' is ahead of you.
9. Continue along the wide path for about ½ mile. At a crossing of tracks turn right to follow another wide track for about ¼ mile down to the road. You will pass a track and a climbing stone on your right and cross one stile.
10. At the road turn left, to walk round the quarry.
11. Bear right down the hill into Birchover.

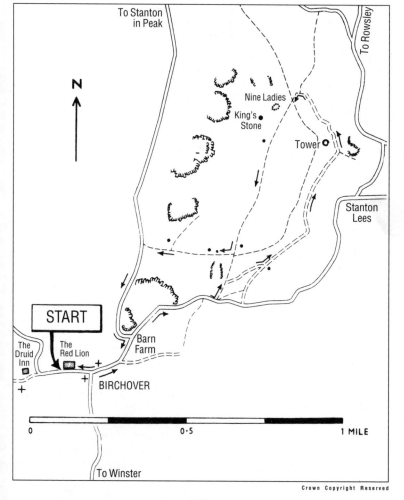

Crown Copyright Reserved

Calver – Stoney Middleton – Coombs Dale – Peak Pasture – Calver

STARTING POINT: *The Derwentwater Arms,* Calver.

PARKING: Near *The Derwentwater Arms,* Calver.
Directions: From the main Calver crossroads, take the residential road, situated between the Bakewell and Chesterfield (A623) roads – Sough Lane. *The Derwentwater Arms* is on the right, and you park on the left side of the wide road.

WALK DESCRIPTION: The village of Stoney Middleton lies at the foot of a narrow limestone cleft, and it is from here, after a short road walk from Calver (pronounced Carver), that this walk commences. You climb a steep road from the village, and then follow fieldpaths which lead over meadows to descend a steep path into Coombs Dale. From this remote, steep-sided valley, you follow another quiet stony dale, and then gradually ascend the hillside. On the track from this point an impressive view opens up, with the villages of Foolow and Eyam in the distance. Further along the track, the view widens to include Froggatt, Curbar, and Baslow Edges. A descending track leads directly to the village of Calver where your walk commenced.

ROUTE INSTRUCTIONS:

1. With *The Derwentwater Arms* behind you, walk to the Calver crossroads, and follow the Manchester A623 road for half a mile.

2. On reaching Stoney Middleton turn left up High Street past *The Moon Inn,* and in 300 yards turn left along Eaton Fold.

3. Just before reaching a modern bungalow, turn right at the signpost 'Footpath'.

4. Walk up a short track following a wall on your right to go through a gateway, then a garden and a wire mesh gate. Keep straight on with a wall on your right

5. Go through a double stile and bear left across the middle of a field, following the signpost 'Coombs Dale', in the direction of a valley of trees.

6. Cross three stiles and three fields, keeping in the same direction.

7. Bear slightly right to descend a steep path following a wire fence on your left to a promontory overlooking the dale.

8. Descend the steep path which is to the right of the promontory. At the bottom of the hill the path turns left under the trees to a stile. Cross this stile.

9. Turn right along the lane and in 300 yards opposite a promontory on your right, turn left by the footpath sign across a plank bridge, a rough grass area and over a stile.

10. Turn right to follow a fence on your right then round a left hand bend. <u>Pass</u> a stile on your right and continue up the valley.

11. At a gate and waymarked post bear up left away from the wall to pass under power lines and then to follow them. Just before a gate and stile turn left onto a wide track.

12. Follow the track with a wall and then a fence on your right. Cross a stile to enter a walled track.

13. Follow this track for just over ½ mile passing through one gate.

14. Cross a stile, and in 100 yards cross another stile. Cross the road diagonally right to Cross Lane.

15. Take the first turn left Shippon Lane, and turn left along 'Lowside' back to *The Derwentwater Arms.*

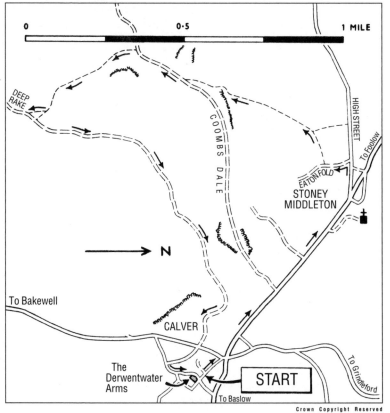

Crown Copyright Reserved

Haywood Car Park – Tumbling Hill – Upper Padley – Grindleford – Hay Wood – Haywood Car Park

STARTING POINT: Haywood Car Park – 2½ miles from Calver.

PARKING: Haywood Car Park.
Directions: To reach the car park from Calver crossroads, take the B6001 Hathersage road, and in 300 yards, turn right onto the B6054 Sheffield via Froggatt Edge road. The car park is on your left in 2½ miles, 300 yards past a left hand bend.

WALK DESCRIPTION: One continually marvels at the unexpected aspects of the Derbyshire countryside one can see from various viewpoints, and this is yet another ridge walk from which there is an extensive view. As you leave the Haywood Car Park and proceed along the narrow undulating ridge path of Jubilee Hill and Tumbling Hill, you see Grindleford in the valley below, with Mag Clough behind, and over to the right, Sherriff Wood, with Eyam Moor in the distance. Still further to the right is Hathersage and Win Hill. From this exhilarating viewpoint you descend through woods to Grindleford Station, where you pass Totley Tunnel, 3½ miles long, and the second longest tunnel in England. From here you pass historic Padley Hall, and descend on field paths to a footpath beside the River Derwent. Crossing the main road at Grindleford, you climb steeply through Hay Wood back to the car park.

ROUTE INSTRUCTIONS:

1. Follow the signpost 'Jubilee Hill' in Haywood Car Park, and cross a stile just past the entrance drive.

2. Turn left on a path keeping along the top of the ridge, taking a right fork then a left fork, and eventually passing the foot of high rocks.

3. Follow a rough undulating stony footpath to a swing gate (do not go through it) and continue along the ridge with a wall on your right (about ¼ mile in all).

4. Follow the path as it descends through woods, and at the T-junction of tracks turn left.

5. At a minor road turn right. Cross the main road and turn right for 40 yards to descend a surfaced path.

6. At Grindleford Station turn right, cross the railway bridge and river bridge to follow the track past Padley Mill and a row of houses on your left.

7. Pass Padley Hall on your right, and in 80 yards, just after crossing a cattle grid, turn left through a kissing gate and cross a railway bridge.

8. Follow the track and 135 yards from the railway bridge, turn left to leave the track by wooden posts and go through a gateway. Proceed diagonally right across the field to the right hand corner.

9. Follow the path, with a wall on your right, then through a marshy area. Go through a kissing gate on your left and turn left.

10. Follow the path with a wall and hedge on your left, to the main road at Grindleford, cross the road and turn right, then left along a track, with the churchyard on your left.

11. Where the track bears right to Haywood Farm, turn left over a stile into Hay Wood.

12. Follow the woodland path uphill, passing through a gate. At the water inspection grate cross a track and continue uphill bearing right. Join a track at a T-junction.

13. Turn right on the track, and pass through a gate to a path which leads to Haywood Car Park.

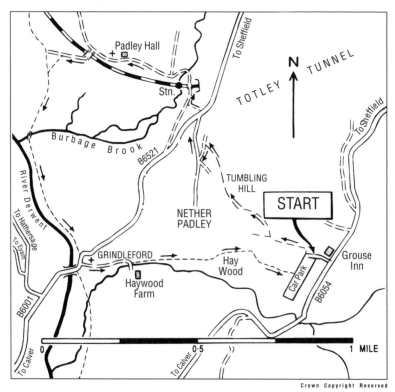

Crown Copyright Reserved

Castleton – Hollowford Road – Hollins Cross – Losehill Hall – Castleton

STARTING POINT: Castleton Car Park.

PARKING: Castleton Car Park, on the main road in the centre of the town. Pay and Display.

WALK DESCRIPTION: This scenic ridge walk gives you magnificent views over Edale up to Kinder Scout and across to Win Hill. It is best walked on a clear day. If you wish to climb Back Tor and Lose Hill keep straight on up the ridge after crossing a stile on your left at Point 8. At the viewfinder on the top of Lose Hill bear right downhill to cross a stile by the National Trust sign and continue downhill to cross a stile on your right. Now follow instructions from Point 11. You descend through fields and along tracks back to Castleton.

ROUTE INSTRUCTIONS:

1. Follow the footpath on the eastern Castleton Car Park boundary beside a stream, which leads away from the main road. Turn right at the end of the car park.

2. Walk up a short way between cottages and on reaching a minor road turn left.

3. Follow the twisting Hollowford Road for about 1 mile. After the first ⅓ mile, at the Hollowford Training Centre, bear left and at a T-junction turn left.

4. Where the road turns left, go over a wooden stile.

5. Follow a tree-lined path up the hillside.

6. At a junction of paths and stiles turn left over a stile signed Hollins Cross.

7. Continue up the well-defined path crossing two stiles to Hollins Cross.

8. Turn right along the ridge. After just over ½ mile by a stile on your left keep straight on. (If you wish to follow the Back Tor and Lose Hill route cross the stile, turn right to continue uphill).

9. Cross a stile to walk through open woodland. Cross another stile.

10. Keep straight on up the next four fields crossing three stiles. At the fourth stile turn right (do not cross it).

11. Walk downhill following a fence and broken wall on your left. The path shortly veers away from the fence to pass a small copse and valley on your right.

12. 80 yards past the copse, turn very sharp right at a signpost to walk down the field to cross a stile in the bottom right hand corner.

13. Keep straight on, with a wall on your right, and in 80 yards turn right through two stiles.

14. Cross the field in the direction of Mam Tor, cross a stile by a gate, and keep straight on on a track, with a wall shortly on your right. Cross a stile by a gate.

15. Keep straight on, still in the direction of Mam Tor.

16. Cross two stiles and turn left at the waymark 'Castleton'.

17. Go through a stile on your left at the signpost 'Footpath to Castleton. Please keep to the right side of the field'.

18. At the end of the field by a waymarked post descend to the stream and cross the footbridge, climb steps to go through a gate, and turn left. Cross the bottom of the field and another stile and keep straight on.

19. Go through a gate onto a lane behind Losehill Hall, turn right for 100 yards, and where the lane bends left, keep straight on through a gated stile.

20. Cross the top of the field to go through another gate and across stepping stones.

21. Keep straight on across the field. Turn left over a cattle grid. Follow the track to the Hollowford Training Centre.

22. At the T-junction turn left along the lane.

23. 20 yards past the 'School' sign, turn right to the car park.

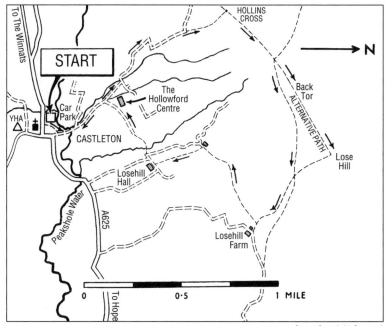

Crown Copyright Reserved

Eyam – Sir William Hill Road – Eyam Moor –
Jubilee Plantation – Highcliffe – Eyam

STARTING POINT: Eyam Car Park.

PARKING: Eyam Car Park. Pay and Display.
Directions: Drive along the main street of Eyam, passing the church on your right and Eyam Hall car park on your left, then the Post Office on your right. Turn right up Hawkhill Road signed 'Car Park'.

WALK DESCRIPTION: As this walk starts from Eyam (pronounced Eem), you will no doubt wish to explore this historic village before setting out on the walk. In 1665 the plague of London was carried to Eyam in a box of damp material, which, on being dried out, released the infection. This quickly spread through the village. The villagers, inspired by their rector William Mompesson, heroically decided to contain the infection within their community, by not having contact with anyone outside the village until the infection had subsided. Their food and medicine was left for them beside Mompesson's Well, which you will pass on this walk at Point 3. Their coins were left in the well to wash away any infection. In Eyam you will see the cottage where the plague started, and many other cottages with plaques showing the names of the occupants who died. The heroism of the villagers resulted in the infection being confined to Eyam. You will also be interested to see the elegant mansion – Eyam Hall, the Sheep Roast, and the church, with its ancient sundial and Celtic cross. On this easy walk you have fine views over Eyam, Hathersage and Stanage Edge.

ROUTE INSTRUCTIONS:

1. Turn right out of Eyam Car Park and follow the road round a right-hand bend.

2. Pass the Youth Hostel on your left and follow the road round a left-hand bend.

3. Pass a road on your left and keep straight on at the signpost 'Grindleford', passing Mompesson's Well on your left.

4. At a right-hand bend in the road, with a walled track, Sir William Hill Road to the left, cross the left-hand stile signed 'Public footpath via Stoke Ford to Abney'.

5. Follow the path, with the wall on your right, across the moor. It eventually bears left, and 50 yards before reaching a stile and gate turn left. With a wall close on your right, follow a wide grass path.

6. After nearly ¼ mile, turn right over a stile by a gate.

7. Continue to follow the path with the wall on your right, first through open woodland then round a left hand bend. Cross a stile by a gate.

8. Keep straight on with a wall still on your right and a broken wall on your left.

9. Pass through a wide wall gap and keep straight on to pick up a farm track. Follow this track which will shortly have a wall and the rhododendrons on the right.

10. Cross a ladder stile and turn left along a walled track.

11. At the road turn left, and follow the road in a right bend.

12. Follow the road round a left-hand bend and a double bend round Trap House, and in 100 yards, by railings, bear right down a narrow walled track, to join a minor road.

13. At the T-junction turn right to the car park.

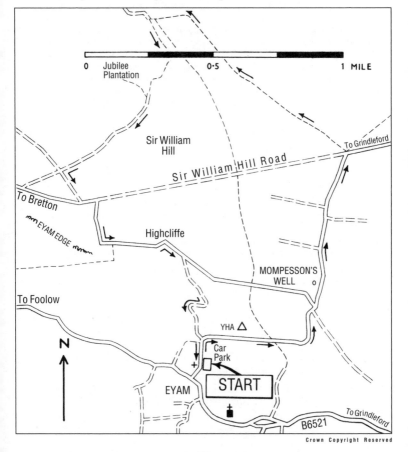

Crown Copyright Reserved

Eyam – Riley Graves – Stoney Middleton – Eyam

STARTING POINT: Eyam Car Park.

PARKING: Eyam Car Park. Pay and Display.
Directions: Drive along the main street of Eyam, passing the church on your right and Eyam Hall car park on your left, then the Post Office on your right. Turn right up Hawkhill Road signed 'Car Park'.

WALK DESCRIPTION: The history of the plague village of Eyam is outlined in Walk 16, and further interesting information is available in the church. On this walk more evidence of the plague period can be seen at the Riley Graves, at Point 4, where John Hancock and his six children are buried, having all died within a week. Mrs. Hancock, the only surviving member of the family, dragged the bodies into the field and buried them. At Point 10 you pass the Boundary Stone, which is indented with six holes. Here money was left in return for food supplied by the residents in nearby villages. This route takes you through Eyam to the Riley Graves, and then along a woodland path to the Eyam-Grindleford road, from which you descend a very rough track to Stoney Middleton. You pass the unusual octagonal church, and eventually climb out of Stoney Middleton up a steep hillside. On reaching Eyam you retrace your route back to the car park.

ROUTE INSTRUCTIONS:

1. Turn left out of Eyam Car Park, and left at the T-junction.

2. Walk along the main village street for nearly ½ mile, and at the junction keep straight ahead on the Hathersage road.

3. In ¼ mile bear left at a 'No Through Road' sign, and 'No Turning Space' signposted 'Riley Graves'.

4. Climb the hill and bear right at the signboard 'Riley Graves' onto a gravel track, passing the graves enclosure, and on reaching a wood on your right, bear right down a path signed 'Public footpath'.

5. Follow the wide path through the wood and after about 200 yards the path goes round a left bend and down a short fairly steep bank at the bottom of which leave the main path to turn right. Follow a narrow path downhill. Eventually, as you leave the wood, you enter a very short walled path. Cross a stile by a gate. Walk down the field keeping a wall close on your left. Pass through a stile by a gate.

6. Cross the road diagonally left and turn right by the black and white bend sign. Follow a walled track downhill for about ¼ mile.

7. At the bottom of the track follow the road in right, left and right hand bends, past Stoney Middleton church, and turn right up 'The Bank'.

8. At a 'No Through Road' sign, bear right and then left up a lane signed 'Cliff Bottom leading to Mill Lane' and 'Eyam'.

9. Just after a sign 'Unsuitable for motor vehicles' turn left over a stile at the signpost 'Public footpath to Eyam 1½'.

10. Follow the steep path up the hillside, aiming for a stand of trees up on your right. Pass the Boundary Stone, on your right.

11. Go through a stile, follow a walled path and pass through a second stile.

12. Continue ahead following a farm track. Pass through a gateway then around a gate to enter a walled track by the houses and farm. Go round a second gate and through another gateway. Keep straight on down the lane.

13. At the main road turn left along Church Street back to the car park.

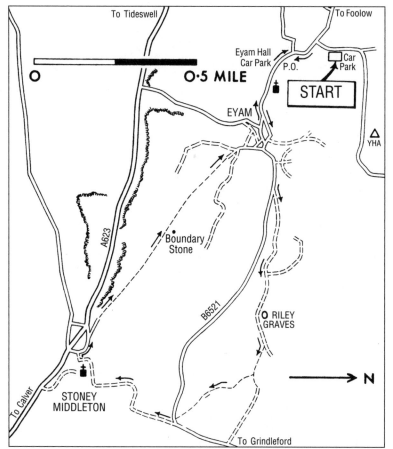

Crown Copyright Reserved

39

Sir William Hill – Bretton Clough – Nether Bretton – Sir William Hill

STARTING POINT: The top of Sir William Hill Road, near Grindleford.

PARKING: The top of Sir William Hill Road, near Grindleford.
Directions: From Grindleford, take the B6001 Hathersage road.
In 200 yards take the first turn left, and in 1¼ miles, where the road
bends left, keep straight on (with care) into a rough walled lane.
Park where convenient (Sir William Hill Road).

WALK DESCRIPTION: This scenic walk, through a lovely wooded area of
the Peak Park, takes you away from busy roads, to enjoy the stillness we all seek
on our excursions into the countryside. At the start of the walk, along a moorland
path, you have an extensive view on your right of Stanage Edge and Higger Tor,
leading on to Hathersage, the Hope Valley, Win Hill, Lose Hill and Mam Tor.
At Point 3 you see Bretton Clough lying below. You continue your walk along
Bretton Clough, and climb a steep winding path to Nether Bretton. Tracks lead
you back to your parking area.

ROUTE INSTRUCTIONS:

1. Go over the left-hand stile signed 'Public footpath via Stoke Ford to Abney'.
2. Follow the path, which at first runs near the wall and eventually veers to the left.
3. Go over a stile to follow a wide ridge path with a wall on your right. Cross a
   wall stile. Shortly the path veers away from the wall downhill, and round a
   left hand bend as you approach the trees.
4. Follow the well-defined path downhill, ignoring paths off to the right then off
   to the left, to a T-junction. Turn left to follow the main path gradually uphill.
5. Cross a stile and, shortly after crossing a stream, climb a steep field with a
   broken wall on the left. Keep straight on crossing five broken walls then
   follow a path through a wood and across a wet area.
6. Continue to follow the path which shortly has a fence on the right.
7. Cross a stile and a stream. Bear right up to a wall and turn sharp left to have
   a wall on your right.
8. Climb the woodland path as it zig-zags up the hill.
9. As you near the top of the hill there is a welcome seat from which there are
   great views.
10. Bear right on up the hill and go over a stile. Walk up towards a cottage, cross
    another stile and continue up a narrow walled path.
11. At the lane, turn left, and follow a wide walled track.
12. On reaching the road, turn left, and in 50 yards, keep straight on along a
    walled rough unsurfaced road signed "Unsuitable for motors". Follow Sir
    William Hill Road for one mile back to your starting point.

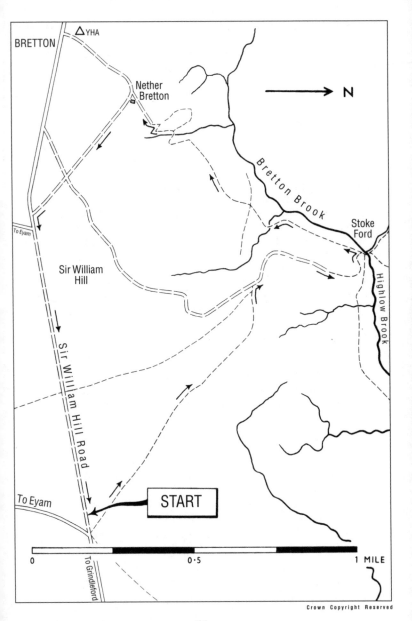

BRETTON

△YHA

Nether
Bretton

To Eyam

Sir William
Hill

Sir William Hill Road

To Eyam

START

Bretton Brook

Stoke
Ford

Highlow Brook

N

0   0·5   1 MILE

To Grindleford

Crown Copyright Reserved

41

Grindleford Station – Upper Padley – Hathersage Booths – Harper Lees – Grindleford Station

STARTING POINT: Grindleford Station approach road.

PARKING: Grindleford Station approach road.
Directions: From Grindleford bridge, take the B6521 Sheffield road, and in ½ mile, just past *The Maynard Arms Hotel*, bear left down the station road. Park where convenient.

WALK DESCRIPTION: A quiet stroll through National Trust property 'Upper Padley', and along a picturesque path by the River Derwent, are the attractions of this walk. As you walk through Upper Padley, Millstone Edge rises steeply on your right, while on your left the view extends from Leadmill Bridge and the River Derwent to Bretton Clough in the distance. This quiet track leads to the main Sheffield to Hathersage road. From this road you cross the railway track and descend to the riverside path, which you follow, through woodland, to re-cross the railway. On the railway bridge a view of Hathersage and Stanage Edge is framed at the point where the railway line disappears into the distance. This is a gentle and relaxing walk, with pleasant, rather than dramatic views.

ROUTE INSTRUCTIONS:

1. From Grindleford Station approach road, cross the railway bridge, pass Padley Mill, and keep straight on to Padley Hall, on your right.

2. Keep straight along a wide track, entering the 'National Trust property of Longshaw Estate', walking through woods, open grassland and farms for about one mile.

3. Go through a gate, and on reaching the main Sheffield to Hathersage road, turn left.

4. Keep on the main road. 150 yards beyond *The Millstone Inn*, turn left immediately after *The Beeches* and opposite Booths Farm entrance at a stone circle signed 'Dakins Barn'. Follow the metalled lane downhill.

5. At Dakin's Barn turn right through a gate signposted 'Footpath' and go through a stile at the bottom right-hand corner of the field.

6. Follow the path, with a wall on your left, and cross a stile on your left.

7. Turn right to follow a wall on your right downhill. Cross the busy railway.

8. Turn left down through the wood with a rail first on the right, then on the left. Go over a stile and turn right by a fence, then left down to the riverside.

9. At the riverside road, turn left.

10. Follow the surfaced driveway going through two gates by two cattle grids. At the buildings turn right to go through a kissing gate. Keep straight on across the meadow as indicated by a waymarked post. Cross a broken wall, Follow the riverside path. Go through a gate into Coppice Wood.

11. Follow the woodland path for about 100 yards then turn left away from the river up a sunken path. In nearly 300 yards turn left again at a Footpath sign.

12. Go through a gate and almost immediately turn left over a railway bridge and through a gap by an old gate.

13. Continue ahead up through the bracken until you reach a stony track. Turn right to retrace your route back to Grindleford Station.

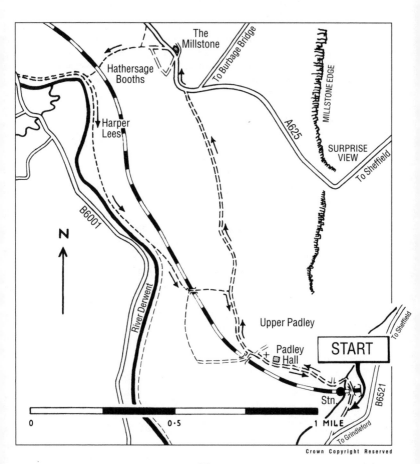

Crown Copyright Reserved

Surprise View Car Park – Millstone Edge – Hathersage – Derwent River – Padley Gorge – Surprise View Car Park

STARTING POINT: Surprise View Car Park.

PARKING: Surprise View Car Park
Directions: From Hathersage, take the A625 Sheffield road, and in 2 miles, just after passing through a rocky cleft, turn left into the car park.

WALK DESCRIPTION: If you are visiting the Peak Park for the first time, the 'Surprise View' will indeed live up to its name, as you reach Millstone Edge at the beginning of this walk. You can enjoy the view all the way along the Edge until you reach a moorland path, from which you descend the valley which leads to the village of Hathersage. You walk through the outskirts of Hathersage to a riverside path alongside the River Derwent, and climb through a wood towards Upper Padley. A walk beside Burbage Brook up the delightful Padley Gorge brings you back to the Surprise View Car Park.

ROUTE INSTRUCTIONS:

1. At the Hathersage end of the Surprise View Car Park near the road, go through a swing gate and follow a path which veers very slightly right across the moor, keeping almost parallel to the road.

2. On reaching a fence along Millstone Edge, turn right, with fence on left.

3. After about ½ mile the land drops steeply down. Just before this descent and by a stile on your left turn right to follow a path down a gentle slope and round to the left.

4. Continue in the same northerly direction for about ½ mile.

5. Where the path reaches a bend in the wall, keep straight on for 150 yards.

6. Bear left down to the road and turn right.

7. In 100 yards go through a gate on your left, turn left to follow a path round a right hand bend and walk down a slope following a wall close on your left.

8. On nearing a stile on your right, bear left and continue down the valley with the wall still on your left and shortly a wall also on your right; go through a gateway or over a stile.

9. Keep to the walled track uphill to the road, turn left. Follow the road for ³/₄ mile.

10. Pass the *Scotchman's Pack,* and at the T-junction turn left on the A625.

11. At the first road on the right, cross the top of Crossland Road and walk along Back Lane.

12. Turn left at the T-junction onto the B6001, walk under the railway bridge, and in ¹/₄ mile, just after a left bend and bridge sign, turn left on a track signed 'Harper Lees – Private Road – Public footpath' and 'Public Footpath to Grindleford avoiding main road'.

13. Follow a surfaced track; cross through two gates by cattle grids. At Harper Lees turn right to go through a kissing gate. Keep straight on across the meadow following the arrows on the waymarked post. Cross a broken wall. Follow the riverside path to Coppice Wood.

14. Go through a small gate. Follow the woodland path. In about 100 yards leave the river and bear left up a sunken path to meet a wall on your left for a short way. Before you reach a gate turn left by a Footpath sign to walk up a steep path.

15. Go through a gate and almost immediately turn left over the railway, and go through a gap by an old gate.

16. Keep straight on up the hill to a track and turn right. Walk through Upper Padley.

17. Pass Padley Hall on your left. After passing a row of cottages on your right and a wooden barn on your left, turn left up a steep track.

18. Pass through a swing gate into Padley Gorge, and keep straight on the main wide path through the woods until it emerges via a gate into open heathland.

19. Follow the stream on your right and when level with a plank bridge bear left up a sunken path which leads in the direction of the centre of a distant wood.

20. On reaching the road, go through a gate and turn left to car park.

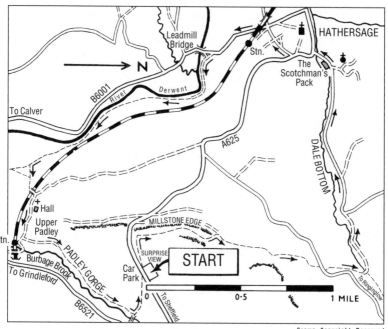

Crown Copyright Reserved

45

Hollin Bank Car Park – North Lees Estate – Dennis Knoll – Stanage Edge – Hollin Bank Car Park

STARTING POINT: Hollin Bank Car Park (beneath Stanage Edge).

PARKING: Hollin Bank Car Park. Pay and Display.
Directions from Hathersage: With *The George Hotel* on your left, follow the A625 Sheffield road, and in ¼ mile, turn left on School Lane. In 1½ miles turn left at the signpost 'Ladybower 5'. Bear right at the signpost 'Ladybower 4', and in ¼ mile turn right into Hollin Bank Car Park.

WALK DESCRIPTION: Contrasting scenery is a feature of this most attractive walk, on which you first meander along the grassy paths of the North Lees Estate, and later cross sweeping moors which rise to the rocky grandeur of Stanage Edge. The walk, if taken on a clear sunny day, has everything – delightful views, crags, streams, picnic spots and clean grassy paths. It starts from a quiet and isolated picnic area and car park lying on the moorland beneath Stanage Edge, where climbers gather to enjoy their sport on these famous gritstone crags. From the North Lees Estate you see the historic sixteenth century North Lees Hall nearby on your left, and the lovely valley leading down to Hathersage. After passing through the farmyard at Green's House, you again reach an excellent viewpoint. If you wish to shorten the walk, turn right along the road at Point 8, and keep straight on for ¾ mile to the car park. To continue the walk you follow a quiet moorland track. A steady climb leads you to the top of Stanage Edge – an exhilarating viewpoint – and you descend from there, down the Roman pathway back to the car park.

ROUTE INSTRUCTIONS:

1. Turn left out of Hollin Bank car park. In about 200 yards turn right over a stile at the end of the Mountain Rescue Building and Toilets. Follow the stepped path down through the wood. At a T-junction turn right to follow a wide stony track.

2. Cross a stile by a gate, and immediately bear right on a path leading away from the main track.

3. Keep straight on at the waymarked stone and in 40 yards go over a stone and ladder stile and turn left on a wide path down the hillside.

4. Follow the path round a double bend passing a gate and footpath post. Cross a stile and stepping stones over a stream. Follow the waymarked path uphill to the left.

5. Cross a stile and continue ahead crossing two fields, one stile and an improvised gate. Turn left up a walled grass track to go through a gate to Green's House Farm (converted).

6. In 30 yards turn right through a gate at the 'Footpath' sign and then cross a stile.

7. Follow the path with a wall on your right and shortly bear right through a gateway. Continue ahead with the wall on your left. Cross a stile and follow the wall, still on your left, to the road.

8. On reaching the road, turn left for 200 yards, and turn right through the Dennis Knoll car park on a track at the 'Boundary of Open Country' sign.

9. Follow the track diagonally right across the hillside, and on reaching the second of two more 'Boundary of Open Country' signs, leave the track and bear right over a wooden stile and follow a track along the edge.

10. Opposite the first rocky outcrop on your left, turn right down the stone and rock slabbed (Roman) path. Go through a gate, continue on downhill through another gate. In a few yards bear right to the car park at the foot of the hill.

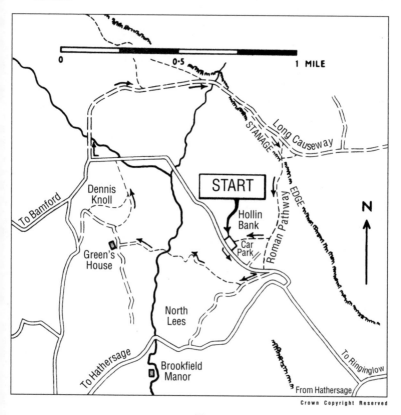

Crown Copyright Reserved

47

Hathersage – Hazelford Hall – Eyam Moor – Stoke Ford – Highlow Wood – Hathersage

STARTING POINT: Hathersage Car Park.

PARKING: Hathersage Car Park. Pay and Display.
Directions: Take the B6001 Grindleford road, opposite *The George Hotel*, for 300 yards. Turn left, and the car park is on your left.

WALK DESCRIPTION: There are some rather steep lanes and paths to climb at the beginning of this walk, in order to reach the high moorland track known as Eyam Moor. You pass the charming seventeenth century Hazelford Hall, and climb a very steep field, where time can be taken to turn around for the view of Hathersage, which lies between the Bamford and Stanage Edges. You cross Eyam Moor, with a view of Higger Tor and Millstone Edge on your left. Further along the path you see Froggatt, Curbar and Baslow Edges lying to the right of Grindleford. You reach the top of Sir William Hill Road, and descend a scenic path to a pretty picnic spot beside Stoke Ford. On this path the scene changes – on your right is Hathersage – ahead is Win Hill. Below lies the tree-filled Bretton Clough. You follow the path along a moorland slope to enter Highlow Wood, which leads you to lanes and the main road back to Hathersage. *The Plough Inn* at Leadmill bridge, with its attractive beer garden is a good refreshment stop.

ROUTE INSTRUCTIONS:

1. Turn right out of the car park, and left at the T-junction along the main Hathersage to Grindleford road.
2. Take the first turn right along Dore Lane passing under the railway, and where the lane turns right, at the gate of Nether Hall, turn left over a waymarked stile.
3. Keep straight on along the footpath with a fence close on your right to Leadmill Bridge on the main road.
4. Turn right across the bridge, passing *The Plough Inn* on your left and take the second road on your right.
5. Just past Hazelford Hall, either follow the lane round a hairpin bend and keep straight on, or go through a stile on your left, and take a short-cut up a steep field, entering a sunken path before crossing a stile. Join the road and keep straight on.
6. In ¼ mile go over a stile on your right opposite the second farm and a stone barn.
7. Follow the path, first with a wall on your left, and then diagonally cross Eyam Moor for one mile.

8. On reaching Sir William Hill Road, cross a stile, turn right, and immediately cross a wall stile on your right signed 'Public footpath via Stoke Ford to Abney'.

9. Follow the well-defined path across the moor, which eventually turns left and descends to a stile by a gate. Cross the stile.

10. Follow a wide grass path along the ridge. Cross a stile. The path shortly veers away from the wall on your right; it descends in a curve and near the valley bottom turns right (there are two right turns either will lead to Stoke Ford).

11. At Stoke Ford bear right away from the bridge up the hillside.

12. Follow the undulating moorland path crossing a stream then a stile by a gate. Now follow a fence on your left to cross another stile by a gate.

13. Descend on a wide track to and through a wood.

14. Cross a small stream and go over a stile, keeping straight on, through a conifer and birch area.

15. Cross a stile and continue in the same direction crossing three fields and going through three gateways. At Tor Farm go through two gates then bear slightly right up the farm drive.

16. On reaching a lane keep straight on, passing Hazelford Hall.

17. At the bottom of the lane turn left along the main road for ½ mile and turn right to the car park.

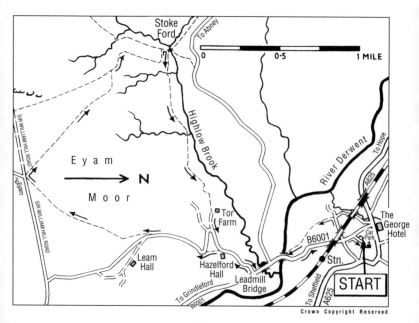

Crown Copyright Reserved

49

Hathersage – Offerton Hall – Callow Wood – Leadmill Bridge – Hathersage

STARTING POINT: Hathersage Car Park.

PARKING: Hathersage Car Park. Pay and Display.
Directions: Take the B6001 Grindleford road, opposite *The George Hotel*, for 300 yards. Turn left, and the car park is on your left.

WALK DESCRIPTION: The beauty of this walk lies in the sweeping lines of hills and valleys to be seen from above Offerton Hall, the highest point of the walk. Shortly after leaving Hathersage, you cross the River Derwent by stepping stones (after heavy rain some of the stones may be under water) at a very pretty stretch of the river, and ascend to Offerton Hall, which lies at the foot of Offerton Moor. Skirting the hillside, you eventually descend, through woodland and field paths, to the banks of the River Derwent, and across Leadmill Bridge to Hathersage.

ROUTE INSTRUCTIONS:

1. Turn right out of the car park (vehicle entrance), and right at the T-junction.
2. On reaching *The George Hotel* at the next T-junction, turn left along the main road for 50 yards, and bear right up Jagger's Lane.
3. Keep straight on until you reach a small stone cottage on the left with a millstone outside.
4. Go through a small gate and walk diagonally right down the field to a stile.
5. Cross the railway by two ladder stiles.
6. Bear diagonally right across a field and over a stile to the main road. Cross the main road to the footpath post. Go through a gated stile.
7. Bear diagonally right across the field, and follow the path beside the Derwent.
8. You will eventually see a waymarked post and stile leading to large stepping stones across the river – cross these, and keep straight on, up the hill.
9. Follow the line of an old grass trackway crossing two stiles by two gates, heading uphill towards Offerton Hall.
10. Go through a gate and turn left along a surfaced lane.
11. Follow this lane round a left-hand bend continuing uphill with Offerton Hall on your left. Stay on the lane round another sharp left hand bend. Continue along the lane above Offerton Hall.
12. After about 300 yards and just past a gate on your left turn left over a stile and immediately bear right.

13. Keep on the path which, after 200 yards, crosses a stream and then a stile immediately beyond it.
14. Follow the path with converted farm buildings down on your left.
15. Turn left through the yard and go through the small gate ahead.
16. Go down through two small fields, and pass through a gate into a wood. Turn left to follow the woodland path.
17. Leave the wood, via a stile, and descend a field to go through a gate.
18. Turn right up the farm drive, and where it meets a surfaced lane, turn left over a stile by a gate opposite the Mount Pleasant Farm drive.
19. Descend the field diagonally right to a wood on your left.
20. Keeping the wood on your left, go over a stile by a gate and continue along the path.
21. Cross a wall stile, and follow a path on down a steep slope.
22. Pass an old stile and a line of broken fence posts down to the river. Turn right to follow the river on your left.
23. At the main road, turn left over Leadmill Bridge, and then immediately left through a waymarked stile.
24. Follow a path with a fence on your left crossing two stiles.
25. Cross a stile by a house, and turn right along a lane.
26. Turn left at the main road, and take the first turn right to the car park.

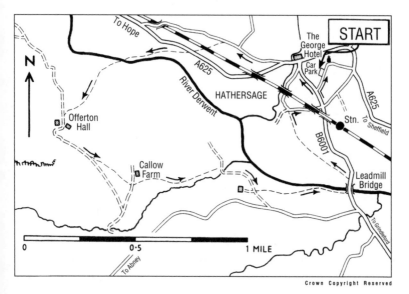

Crown Copyright Reserved

51

Hope – Oaker Farm – Fiddle Clough – Edale End (National Trust) – Guide Post – Fullwood Stile Farm – Hope

STARTING POINT: Hope Car Park.

PARKING: Hope Car Park, adjacent to *The Woodroffe Arms*.

WALK DESCRIPTION: As you start your walk along the Vale of Edale, the hills enclosing the valley rise to Lose Hill on your left and Win Hill on your right. Following tracks and footpaths along the valley, you eventually cross the River Noe, and enter the National Trust area 'Edale End'. As you proceed along a wild moorland path, with the narrow and remote Jagger's Clough lying far below, you have a fine view of the Mam Tor ridge on your left. Shortly you reach the old Roman road, and the Guide Post, dated 1737, showing directions to Edale, Glossop, Sheffield and Hope. From this elevated viewpoint the sweeping lines of Crook Hill, Win Hill, Lose Hill and the Vale of Edale make a scenic panorama. Descending the moorland tracks, you eventually reach the bridge which spans the River Noe, and return along the road to Hope.

ROUTE INSTRUCTIONS:

1. Turn right out of the car park, with *The Woodroffe Arms* on your right, and turn left at the signpost 'Edale'.

2. Keep straight on, and ¼ mile past *The Cheshire Cheese Inn,* bear left at the 'No Through Road' sign, with 'Ashcroft' on your left and 'Bridge Cottage' on your right.

3. At a junction of roads bear right.

4. Pass 'Underliegh' 'Moorgate' and barns. At the entrance to Oaker Farm, cross two stiles on your left and follow the path which runs beside the trees.

5. Go through a stile, follow the fenced path. Cross another stile.

6. Follow the path ahead to cross a stile by a gate. Continue ahead following the fence on your right. Cross a track and bear gently left continuing round the hill before descending to cross a stile under the trees. Turn right down a track (Fiddle Clough).

7. Pass under the railway, turn right on the main road for 15 yards, and turn left over a stile signed 'Public footpath to Hope Brinks'.

8. Cross the bridge over River Noe, and enter National Trust area 'Edale End'.

9. Walk past the National Trust Information Shelter, turn right through a gate, and immediately left at the signpost 'Public footpath'.

10. Walk up the bridle path ignoring a path off to your right. Cross a stile by a gate. Keep straight on following the yellow waymarked sign and the small stone sign to Crookstone Barn.

11. Gradually climb the hillside. Where the main track bears right uphill keep straight on as indicated by the waymarked post. The path soon starts to climb up through the bracken.

12. Cross a stile and follow a sunken path, and on reaching a mound and broken wall, turn right along a wide track with the wall on your left and a fence on your right. Cross a stile.

13. At the signpost 'Win Hill' and 'Hope', turn right over a stile, and follow the public bridleway.

14. Go through a gate and pass the old stone signpost 'Guide Post (1737)'. The wide bridleway gradually veers away from the conifer wood.

15. Go over the stile ahead of you and continue to follow the main track which is mostly downhill. After about ¾ mile near the end of the track go through a gate.

16. At Fullwood Stile Farm bear right keeping to the road (do not go through the farm) and cross the railway bridge.

17. On reaching the road junction, keep straight on across the bridge. Continue along the road for ¾ mile to Hope, turning right at the church to the car park.

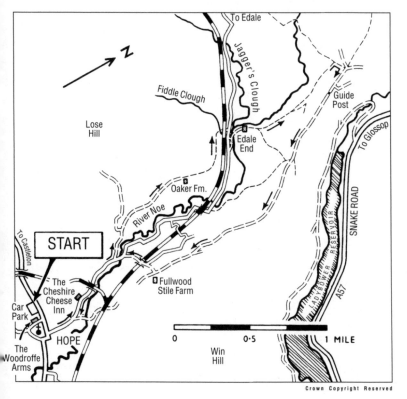

Crown Copyright Reserved

Hope – Brough – Farfield Farm – Killhill Bridge – Hope

STARTING POINT: Hope Car Park.

PARKING: Car Park adjacent to *The Woodroffe Arms,* Hope.

WALK DESCRIPTION: On the last Saturday in June there is a well-dressing festival at Hope followed by a Wakes Week, and at the Summer Bank Holiday weekend, there are Sheepdog Trials and an Agricultural Show, so if you can arrange to take this walk at either of those periods, it will add interest to your outing. On this pleasant and meandering walk around the meadows and lanes surrounding Hope and Brough, you may see an aspect of the Hope valley which is unfamiliar to you. You first take a footpath over the brow of a hill (site of Roman fort, Navio), with views of Win Hill, Lose Hill, and the Mam Tor ridge, to the village of Brough. A walk through the village leads you to the main Sheffield to Hope road, which you cross, near *The Travellers Rest,* to the Aston road. From here footpaths and lanes lead you to Killhill Bridge, where you turn left to Hope.

ROUTE INSTRUCTIONS:

1. Turn right out of Hope Car Park, and then turn right by *The Woodroffe Arms.*
2. Cross the bridge, and take the next turn left up Eccles Lane.
3. In 100 yards turn left over a stile by a gate and bench.
4. Follow the hedge on your left to where it stops then continue ahead up the grass path to go through a squeeze stile by a gate. Continue in the same direction crossing three fields, two stiles and a footbridge and keeping close to the field boundary on your right.
5. Keep straight on across the next field to cross a ladder stile then bear slightly right down the field to go through a gated stile.
6. At the road in Brough turn left.
7. At the T-junction by *The Travellers Rest* turn left and immediately right at the signpost 'Aston'.
8. Cross the railway bridge, and in ¼ mile, opposite 'Round Meadow Barn', turn left over a stile.
9. Bear very slightly left across the field to cross a fence stile, then keep straight on to cross a footbridge.
10. Turn right signposted 'Win Hill'. Keeping in the same direction go over two stiles, and through three gates. Turn left along the lane. Pass roads to Win Hill and Birchfield on your right.
11. Pass Crabtree Cottages and Meadow, on your left, and then, in 100 yards, turn right at Farfield Farm.
12. Bear left at the waymarked stone gatepost and keep on the track passing through a kissing gate and eventually passing under a railway bridge.

13. At the end of the track, turn left to cross Killhill Bridge, and at the T-junction turn left.
14. Follow the road back to Hope, and turn right at the T-junction back to the car park.

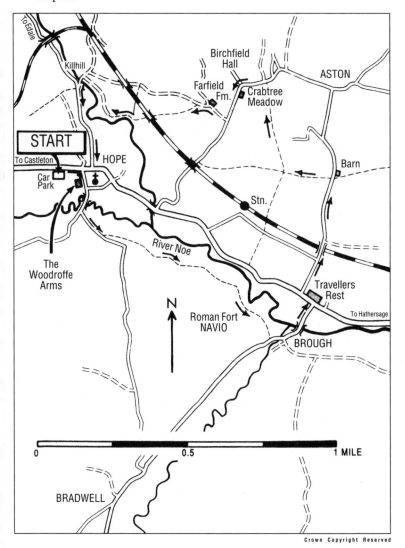

Crown Copyright Reserved

Litton – Tansley Dale – Cressbrook Dale –
Wardlow – Wardlow Mires – Litton

STARTING POINT: The Village Cross, Litton.

PARKING: In Litton.
             No official Car Park.

WALK DESCRIPTION: Although this is one of the shorter walks in the book, it takes you into two beautiful valleys – Tansley Dale and Cressbrook Dale. On the outskirts of the spacious village of Litton, with its large village green and old market cross, you follow paths into these two dales, and a short climb up the steep slopes out of the valley brings you to a point which commands a magnificent view. You soon reach Wardlow along a narrow track, and a short walk along the road to Wardlow Mires takes you round the end of the valley to follow a footpath along the opposite edge. As you return to Litton along this path, you see below the limestone rock, known as Peter's Stone, with Cressbrook Dale curving away into the distance.

ROUTE INSTRUCTIONS:

1. With the village cross on your left, walk along the road signposted 'Wardlow' and take the first turn right, signposted 'Cressbrook, Monsal Dale'.

2. Where the lane bends to the right, turn left, and ignoring the first stile, turn right in 200 yards over a stile.

3. Walk diagonally left to a footpath sign at the wall corner and continue diagonally left down the field to another wall corner, then turn left.

4. Cross a stile and follow the English Nature footpath sign downhill and bearing left. Pass the National Nature Reserve sign and follow the steep path down and into Tansley Dale.

5. At the bottom of the dale cross a gated stile and old bridge pillars then turn right along Cressbrook Dale, bearing left up the hillside in 100 yards.

6. Near the top of the hill, take the left fork to a waymarked stile and the English Nature sign, enter a very narrow field, and keep straight on. Cross a stile and turn right.

7. Follow a walled path. At the main road turn left into Wardlow.

8. Keep straight on, turn left onto the A623, and in 150 yards turn left over a gated stile.

9. Bear right and then follow a path with a wall on your right.

10. Cross a wall stile, bear left across a field to a stile in the corner, and then turn right. Proceed along the path with a wall on your right.

11. Go through a stile and turn left onto the road back to Litton.

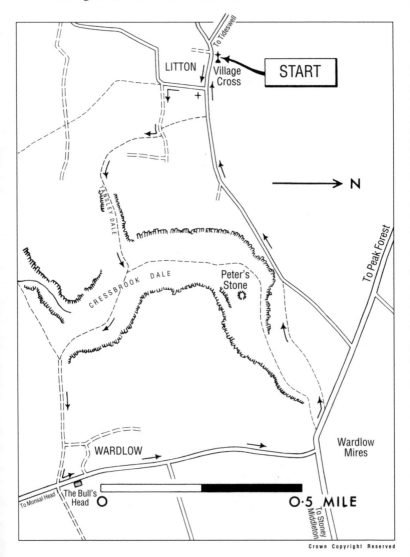

Crown Copyright Reserved

57

Pilsley – Hassop – Birchill Bank Wood – Pilsley

STARTING POINT: Pilsley, near Baslow.

PARKING: On the 'No Through Road', Pilsley.

WALK DESCRIPTION: Although this walk is in a popular part of the Peak District, and not far from Chatsworth Park, it is not well-known, and from the paths and tracks you follow, there are aspects of the countryside you may not have seen before. The walk starts with Pilsley, a quiet village associated with the Chatsworth Estates, and follows a footpath to the main Baslow to Bakewell road. After crossing this road, you ascend, through meadows, to a lane which leads to the hamlet of Hassop, which is dominated by a large Catholic church. You go through a farmyard, which can be very muddy in wet weather, and follow a track to a stream and Birchill Bank Wood, to reach the main road again. From here an enclosed track winds back to Pilsley.

ROUTE INSTRUCTIONS:

1. With *The Devonshire Arms* on your left, follow the road downhill, and in 300 yards turn left over a stile opposite a barn.

2. Follow the path, with a wall on your right, and turn right over a stile near the wall corner.

3. Follow the line of poles down the hillside and cross a bridge over a stream to the main road.

4. Cross the road to another bridge and stile, and ascend the hillside diagonally right.

5. At the top right-hand corner of the field go over a stile by a gate, and follow the path with a wall on your right.

6. Turn a right-hand corner and a left-hand corner and keep straight on with the wall on your right.

7. On reaching a lane, turn left, and keep straight on for 1½ miles to the main road at Hassop, where you turn left at the signpost 'Bakewell'.

8. Keep on the Bakewell road for about 300 yards, and just past a farm on your left, bear left up a track signposted "Unsuitable for motors". Cross a farm track, via two gates and walk up a walled track.

9. Go through a gate and continue ahead on the farm track keeping a fence and then a wall on your right. Pass through a gate and go down a walled track.

10. Cross a stone bridge over a stream and bear left up the hillside.

11. You will walk through woodland then scrubland on a well defined track. Pass through a gate to cross a meadow, and cross a stile to the main road.

12. Turn right for 80 yards, and turn left almost opposite a lay-by onto a track, shortly passing through a gate, and entering a walled track.

13. Keep on this track as it eventually bends sharply to the right, and at the T-junction of paths turn left, back to Pilsley.

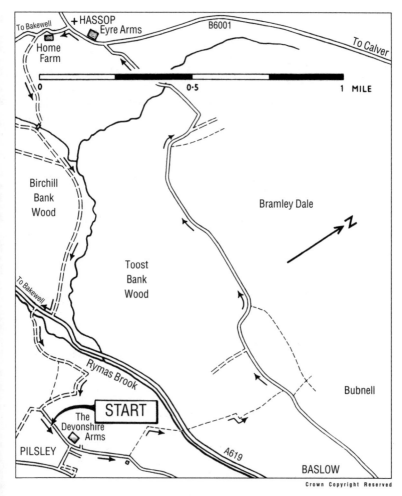

Crown Copyright Reserved

Wormhill – Hargatewall – Peter Dale – Wormhill

STARTING POINT: Wormhill, on the 'No Through Road' leading to the church.

PARKING: As above.

WALK DESCRIPTION: A stroll through Peter Dale, one of the lesser-known dales of the Peak Park, is the object of this walk. Starting from the lane leading to Wormhill church, you soon pass an ornate well, which is in memory of a local resident, James Brindley, the engineer and canal builder. Shortly you encircle Hargatewall and see the strange formation of rocks in Peter Dale in the distance. As you make your way along the rocky path in Peter Dale, you may, if you are a botanist, see rare plants and flowers in this National Nature Reserve. At the end of the valley, a short, steep climb up the hillside leads to tracks, from which can be seen the rocks of Millers Dale. Field paths lead back to the church from which the walk commenced. This walk is best done in the Spring.

ROUTE INSTRUCTIONS:

1. Turn right out of the 'No through road', and walk through the village of Wormhill.

2. In ½ mile, where the road turns left, keep straight on along a minor road in the hamlet of Hargatewall. Where the lane bends left turn right. Ignore the Footpath sign and fork left along a track through the farm buildings. You will pass a large stone barn on your left.

3. At the end of the farm buildings turn right to go through a gate. In about 200 yards there may be another gate to go through across the track, then just past a very small copse of trees cross a stile on your right.

4. Turn left to walk down the field towards the left hand end of a wood and a power-line pole. Cross the wall stile by the pole.

5. Veering slightly left, go over a stile by a gate.

6. Walk down the field with a wall on your right, and go over a stile in the field corner.

7. Turn left then almost immediately right down and up to cross the top of a small valley. Continue ahead to meet a wall on your right. Shortly you will enter a partially walled grass stone track.

8. At the foot of the track, go over a stile and turn right on the lane.

9. In 70 yards turn right over a stile into Peter Dale, at the signpost 'Millers Dale'.

10. Walk down Peter Dale and enter the National Nature Reserve.

11. On reaching the road, turn right, and in 50 yards turn left through a gate.

12. Climb the hillside to an old wall, hawthorns and a fence on your right and go through the stile or gate into a walled track.

13. Follow the track gradually uphill to meet a wall ahead of you. Turn right to continue up the walled grass track. In about 150 yards cross a stile by a small gate and turn left over another stile to follow a wider grass track; this shortly narrows.

14. At the end of the walled track keep straight on to a gated stile.

15. Keep straight on across the middle of the field to a gate at the foot of the field, and turn left over a stile. Continue on a short track.

16. Go through a gateway and turn right on a track leading to the road and back to your starting point.

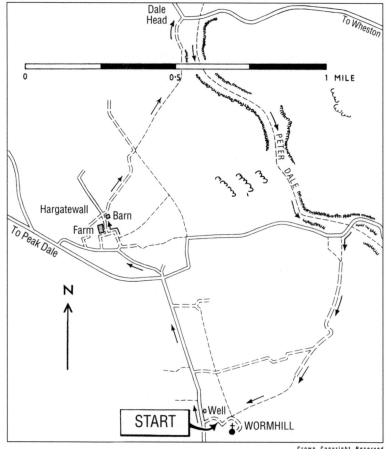

Crown Copyright Reserved

61

Moor Lane Car Park – Middleton – Bradford Dale –
Youlgreave – Moor Lane Car Park

STARTING POINT: Moor Lane Car Park and Picnic Site, near Youlgreave.

PARKING: As above.

Directions from Youlgreave: With Youlgreave church on your left, keep straight on the Newhaven road, and in $1\frac{1}{2}$ miles bear right on the Monyash road. Turn right at the crossroads, right at the T-junction, and right in 100 yards. Moor Lane Car Park is on the right in 150 yards.

Directions from Bakewell: From Bakewell take the B5055 Monyash road, and just past Bakewell church turn left along Yeld Road. Keep straight on this road for 2 miles, and descend a hairpin bend to Conksbury Bridge. Keep straight on for a further $1\frac{1}{2}$ miles, following the Newhaven signpost, and turn left at a 'Picnic' sign to the Moor Lane Car Park. Pay and Display.

WALK DESCRIPTION: In the limestone area of the Peak Park lies the lovely Bradford Dale, extending from Middleton to Youlgreave. The path you take runs alongside the very pleasant picnic area adjacent to the car park, and follows field paths to the village of Middleton. You descend a rather dank woodland track to Bradford Dale, and walk beside the clear water of the River Bradford. The beauty of this riverside walk is enhanced by several dams, which show a pretty pattern of weeds through the clear water. After passing cottages perched on the ridge overlooking the dale, you cross the river over an ancient clapper bridge, and climb a lane from Youlgreave to the car park.

ROUTE INSTRUCTION:

1. Leave the Moor Lane Car Park by the side gateway, turn right to follow the track, passing the picnic site on your right.

2. At the end of the track cross a stile and bear slightly left.

3. Follow a well-used path which shortly winds its way down through the small limestone outcrops towards the trees.

4. Go through an old wall gap by a stile and continue down the path to the road.

5. Turn left along the road for 80 yards, and turn right through a waymarked stile.

6. Pass through a small wood over a broken wall and down a field. Go over a stile, and turn right along a road.

7. Follow the road for just over ½ mile to walk through Middleton village.

8. Where the main road widens out and bears right, keep straight on passing a row of cottages and a house on your left and take the first turn left, by a small grass island. Walk down a rough road which leads into a track.

9. At the bottom of the hill bear left on the main track, and keep straight on through Bradford Dale, following the river on your left.

10. When you see the houses of Youlgreave on your left, cross the clapper bridge and climb the steep lane into Youlgreave.

11. Cross the main road, go along the road opposite, and at the T-junction turn left.

12. Follow this road for one mile back to the car park.

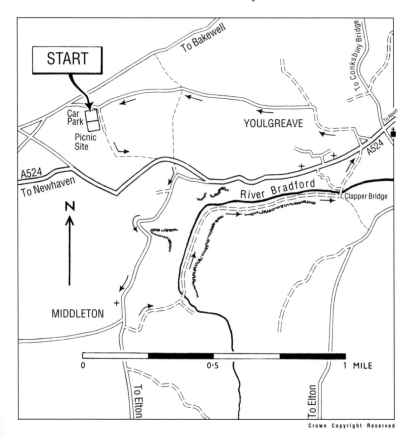

Crown Copyright Reserved

Moor Lane Car Park – Cales Dale – Lathkill Dale –
Meadow Place Grange – Moor Lane Car Park

STARTING POINT: Moor Lane Car Park and Picnic Site, near Youlgreave.

PARKING: As above. Pay and Display. Directions – See Walk 29.

WALK DESCRIPTION: The quiet beauty of Cales Dale and Lathkill Dale can be enjoyed on this walk, which starts from a car park with a very pleasant picnic area in an adjacent field. You cross meadows to Calling Low Farm, and descend on a rather steep, stepped path to Cales Dale. This sheltered valley leads to the middle section of Lathkill Dale, with its scree slopes, wooded banks, weirs and clear water After a one-and-a-half mile walk through the dale, you climb a track through woods to Meadow Place Grange, where, on looking back, you have a view of Over Haddon on the opposite hillside. A gradual ascent through fields takes you back to the car park.

ROUTE INSTRUCTIONS:

1. Turn left out of Moor Lane Car Park. In a few yards cross the main road and go over the gated stile signposted 'Monyash'.
2. Cross a field diagonally and go over a wall stile.
3. Cross the corner of the next field and go over another gated stile.
4. Continue ahead on a path across the centre of the field. Cross a fence stile, then a small field and gate. Go through a small wood.
5. Go over a stile and walk towards Calling Low Farm.
6. Go through a kissing gate signposted 'Diverted Footpath', continue ahead to another gate on your left. Follow the path through the woodland, passing through three more gates.
7. Keep straight on to another small gate signposted 'Diverted Footpath' (marking end of diversion).
8. Walk down the middle of the next three fields passing through three small ` gates.
9. Descend a steep, stepped path into Cales Dale.
10. Cross a stile, climb the bank, and turn right.
11. At Lathkill Dale, cross the bridge and turn right.
12. Follow the dale for 1$^1/_2$ miles, crossing three stiles and on reaching a house, turn right, and cross the footbridge.
13. Turn left to follow the track uphill on a hairpin bend through Meadow Place Wood.